D0210893

How to Be Perfectly Unhappy

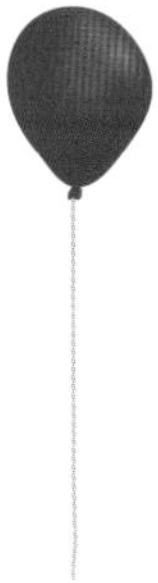

Other books by The Oatmeal

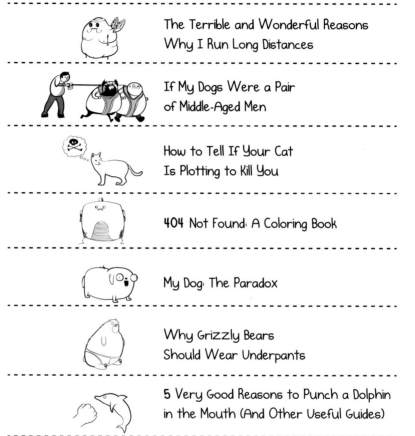

The Terrible and Wonderful Reasons
Why I Run Long Distances

If My Dogs Were a Pair
of Middle-Aged Men

How to Tell If Your Cat
Is Plotting to Kill You

404 Not Found: A Coloring Book

My Dog: The Paradox

Why Grizzly Bears
Should Wear Underpants

5 Very Good Reasons to Punch a Dolphin
in the Mouth (And Other Useful Guides)

www.TheOatmeal.com

How to Be
Perfectly
Unhappy

The Oatmeal

Andrews McMeel
PUBLISHING®

Andrews McMeel Publishing
a division of Andrews McMeel Universal
1130 Walnut Street, Kansas City, Missouri 64106

www.andrewsmcmeel.com

17 18 19 20 21 SDB 10 9 8 7 6 5 4 3 2 1

ISBN: 978-1-4494-3353-6

Editor: Patty Rice
Designer/Art Director: Diane Marsh
Production Editor: Erika Kuster
Production Manager: Tamara Haus

ATTENTION: SCHOOLS AND BUSINESSES
Andrews McMeel books are available at quantity discounts with bulk
purchase for educational, business, or sales promotional use. For
information, please e-mail the Andrews McMeel Publishing Special Sales
Department: specialsales@amuniversal.com.

This book is dedicated to Bryce, Nick, and Sierra,
for all the years you've endured me,
your most misanthropic sibling.

I am not a happy person.

When I tell people this,
they infer that I am
unhappy.

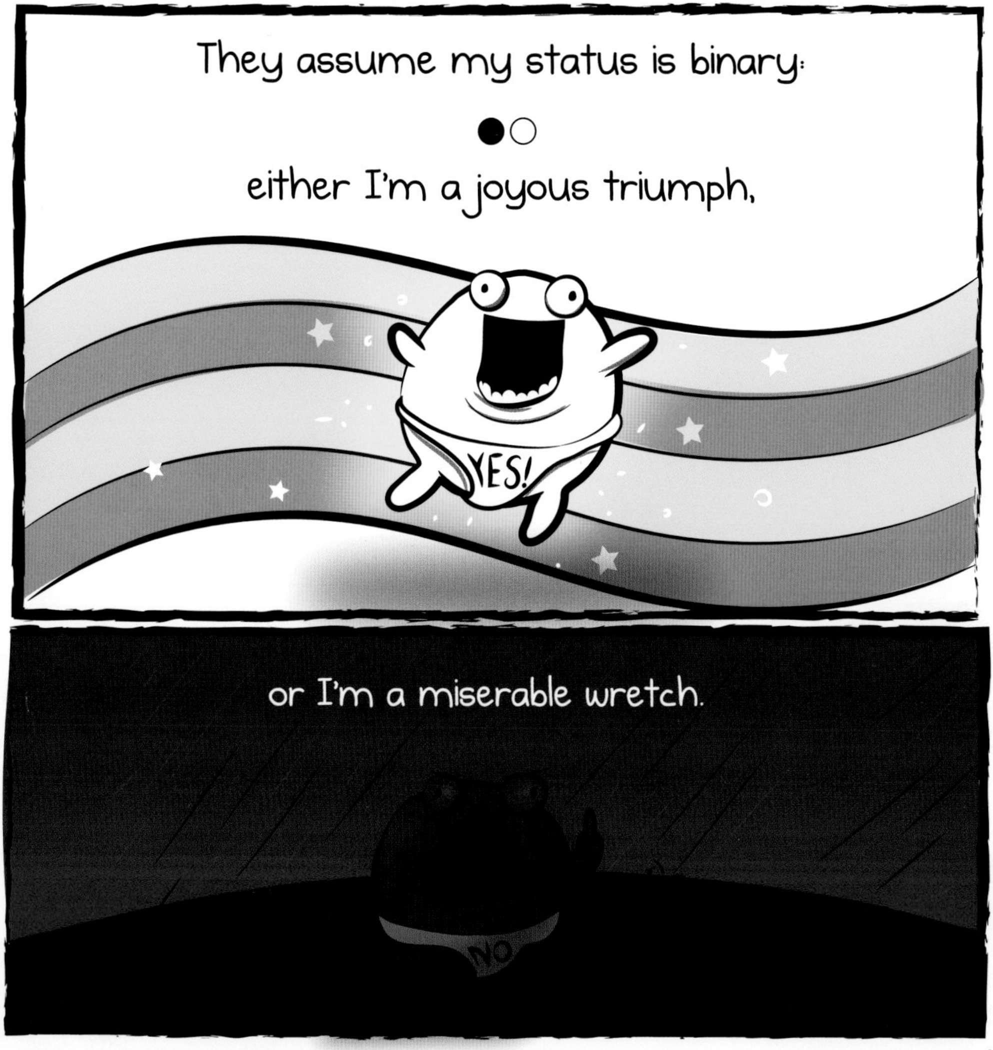
They assume my status is binary:
●○
either I'm a joyous triumph,
YES!
or I'm a miserable wretch.
NO

They recognize no spectrum,
only two states of being:

happy

and

unhappy.

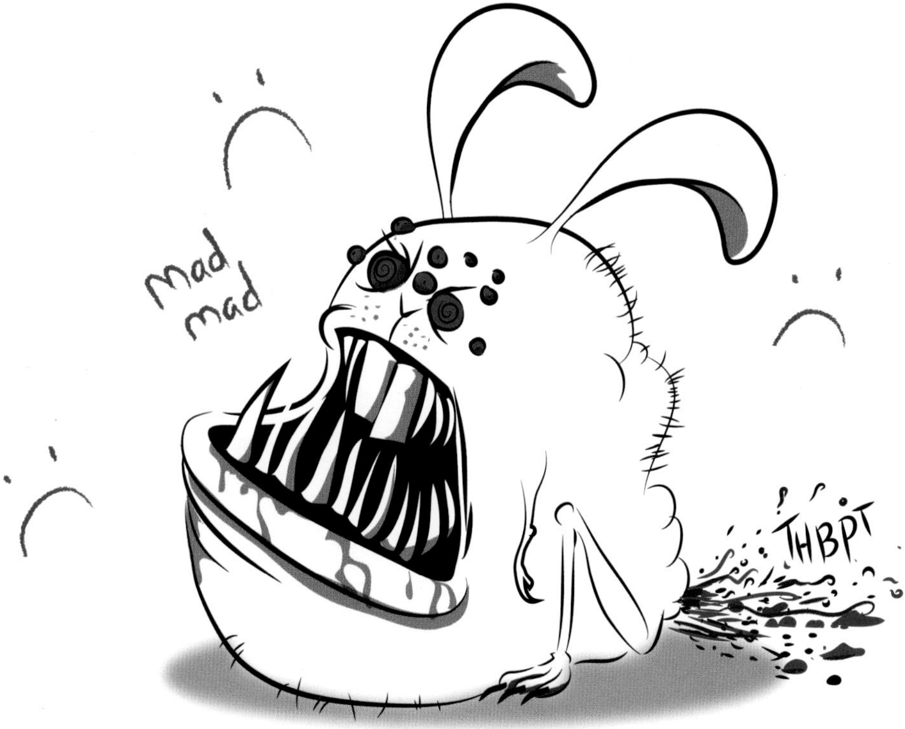

mad
mad
THBPT

But I've never felt "happy."

I've felt joy. I've felt bliss.

But those feelings are ephemeral.

Being "happy" implies permanence.

It implies you completed all the prerequisites.

And now you get to sit atop your giant pile of happy,

forever.

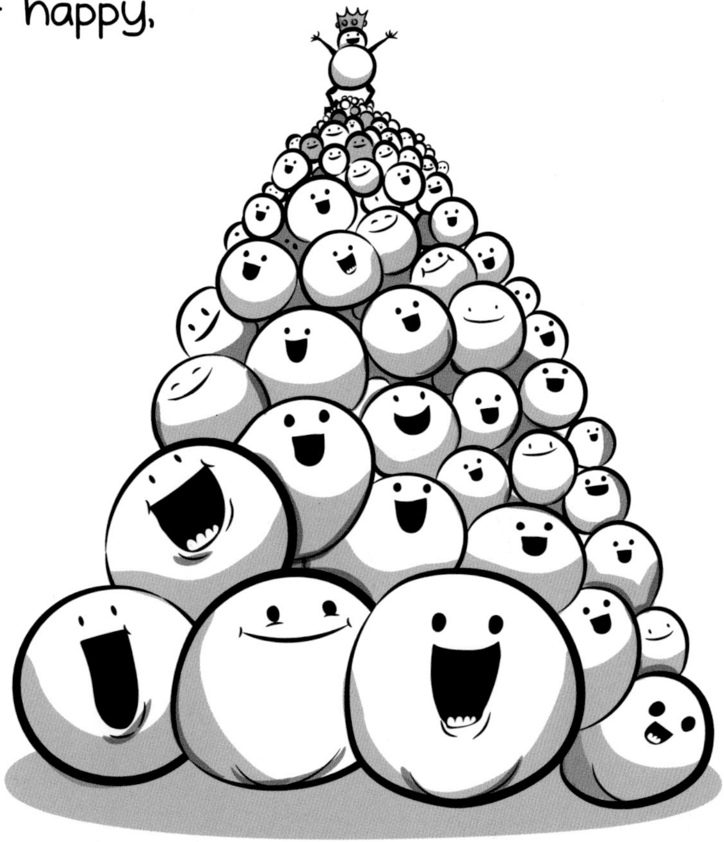

It implies you won.

You beat the end boss.

You made it.

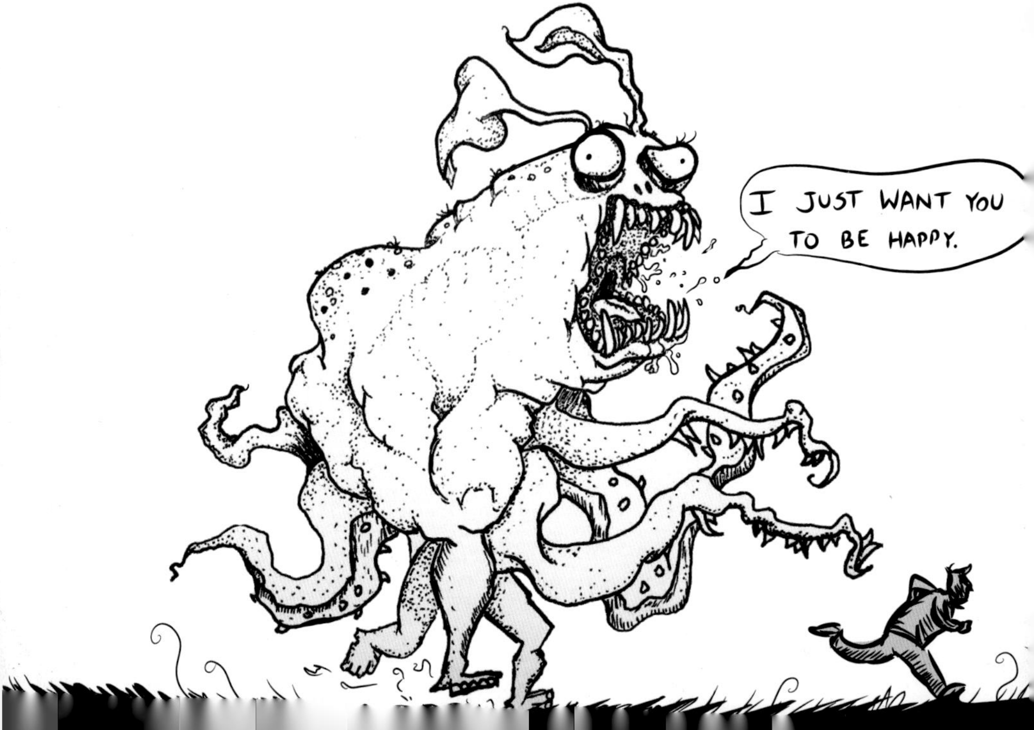
I JUST WANT YOU TO BE HAPPY.

You're a triumph.

You're incredible.

You're *whole.*

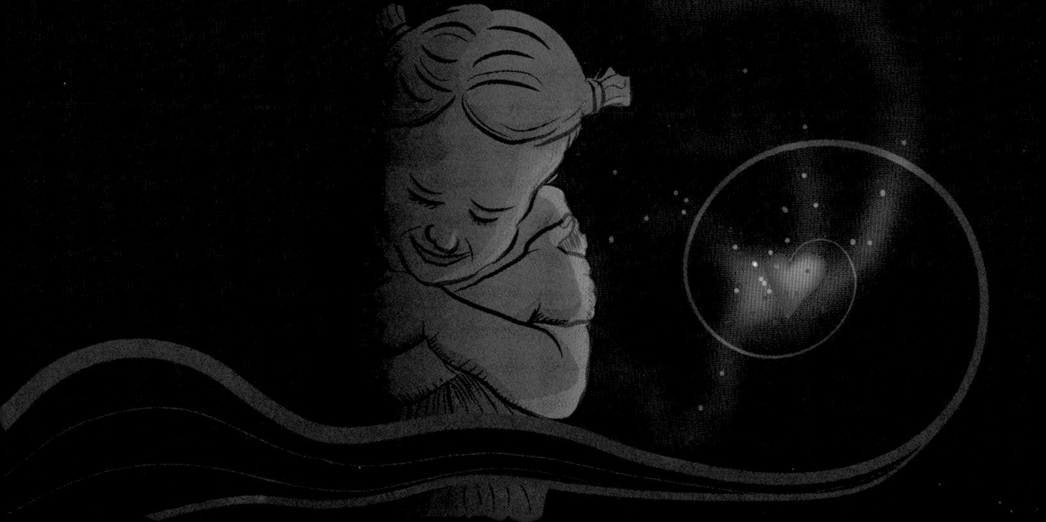

When I disparage this idea of happiness, the counterargument is always the same:

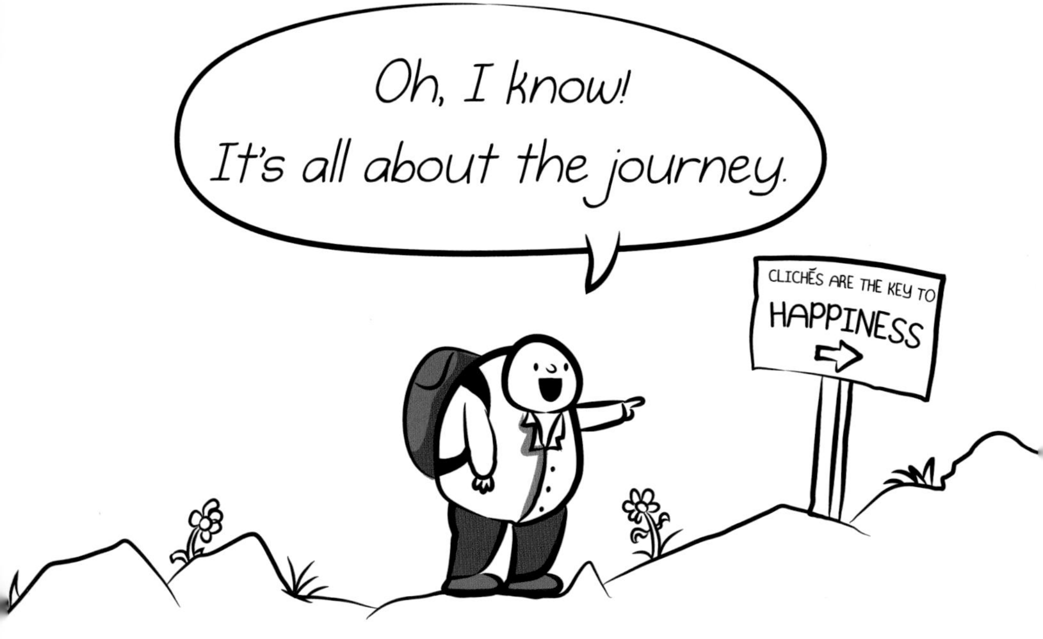
Oh, I know!
It's all about the journey.
CLICHÉS ARE THE KEY TO
HAPPINESS

But that's not it, either.

The conversation about "the journey" is always coupled with the idea that the journey is a joyous one, rich with smiles and fun and laughter.

Also, journeys require endpoints, otherwise you're not Frodo, you're just a homeless guy wandering around with stolen jewelry.

The problem with "happy" is a lot like the problem with Pluto.

Several years ago, Pluto lost its designation as a planet, which caused a lot of uproar.

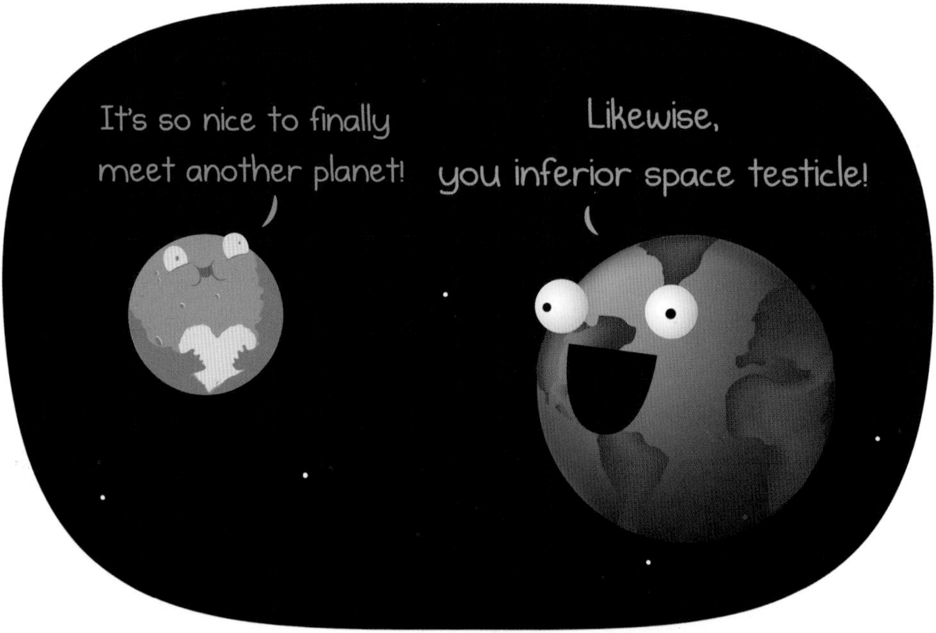
It's so nice to finally meet another planet!
Likewise, you inferior space testicle!

But Pluto itself was never the problem. It's our definition of "planet" that was the problem. "Planet" comes from a Greek word, meaning "wanderer," and was used to describe bodies that move in the sky against a fixed background of stars.

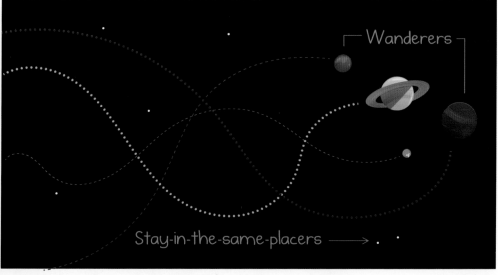

Wanderers

Stay-in-the-same-placers ———→ .

It was a vague way of describing a complex thing.

Does a planet move in a fixed orbit around the sun?

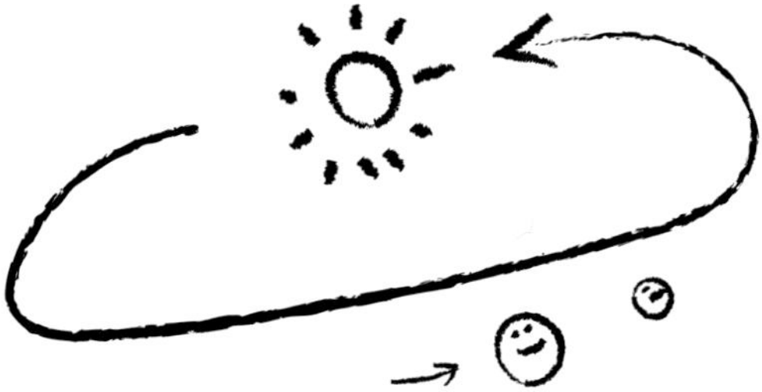

Does it clear a path within that orbit?

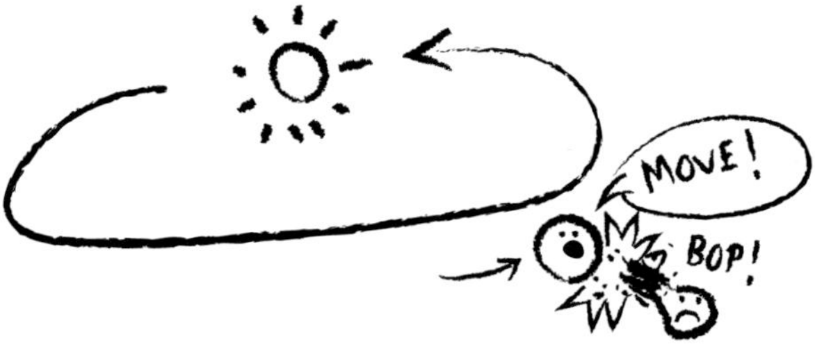
MOVE!
BOP!

Does it have moons?

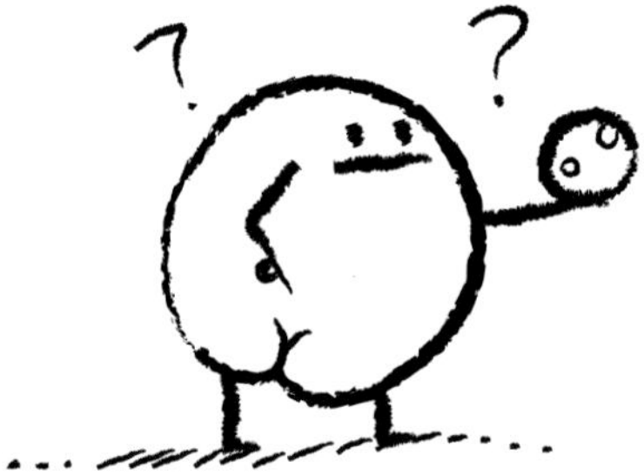

Does it have to be a certain size?

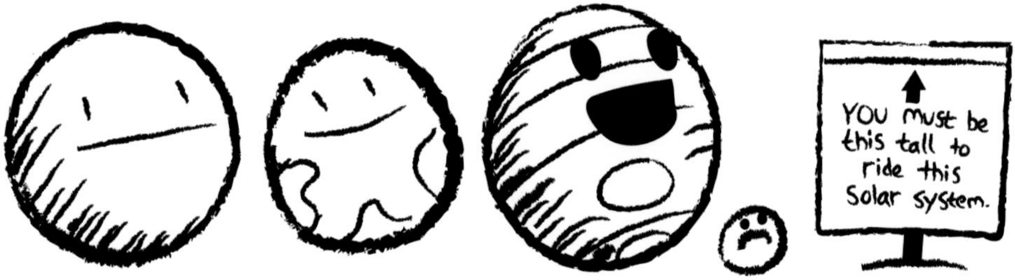
YOU must be this tall to ride this Solar System.

These were the questions that arose
when we clarified our definition of
"planet." These were the smart
questions that got Pluto downgraded.

Pluto is no longer a planet because our
definition of planet wasn't very good.

I'm not "happy" because our definition of
happy isn't very good.

It's a monochromatic word used to describe a rich, painful spectrum of human feeling.

Our sense of happiness is so brittle it can be destroyed simply by asking whether or not it exists.

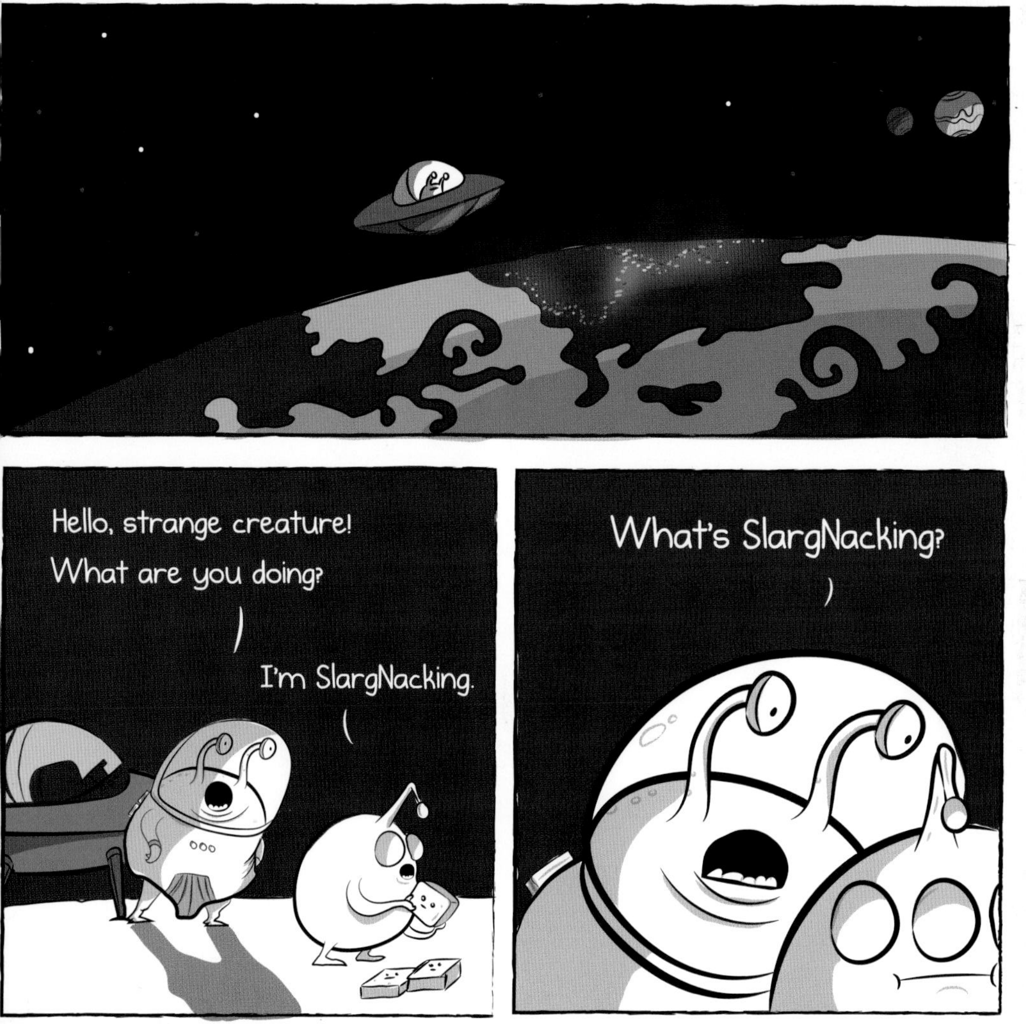
Hello, strange creature!
What are you doing?
I'm SlargNacking.
What's SlargNacking?

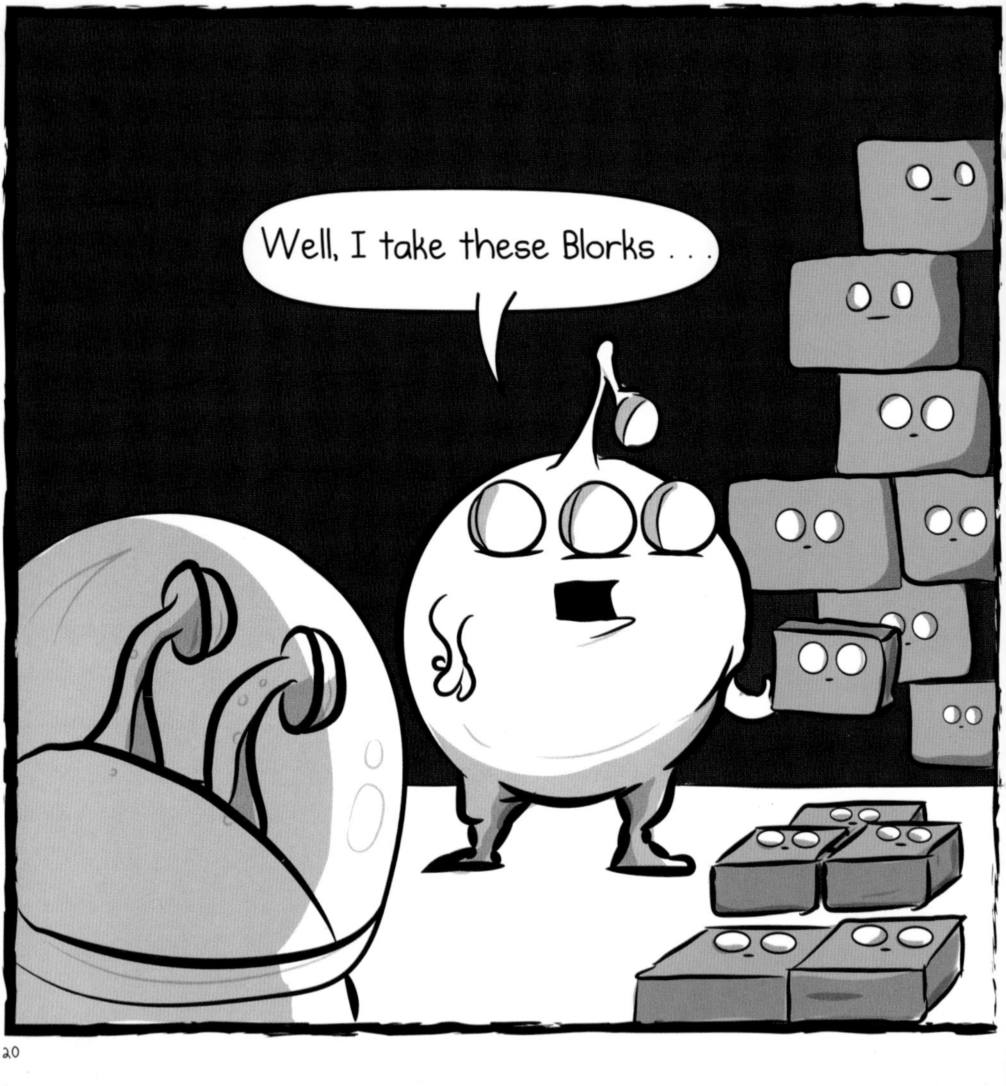
Well, I take these Blorks . . .

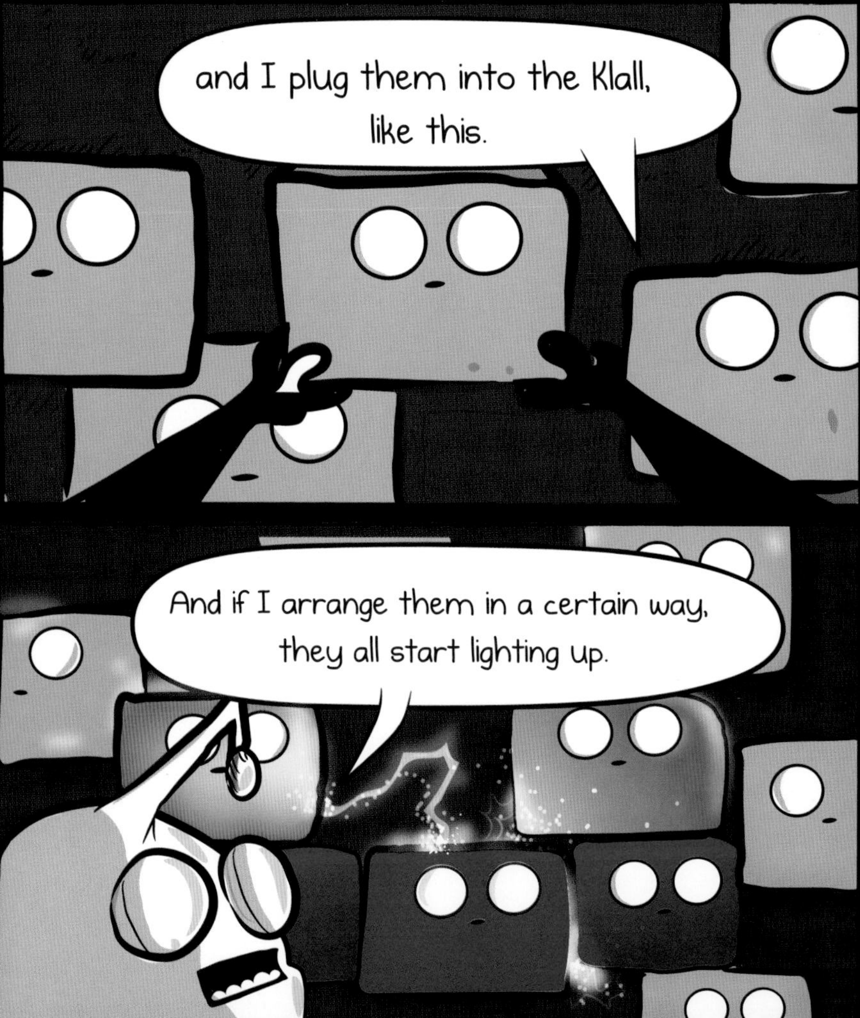
and I plug them into the Klall, like this.
And if I arrange them in a certain way, they all start lighting up.

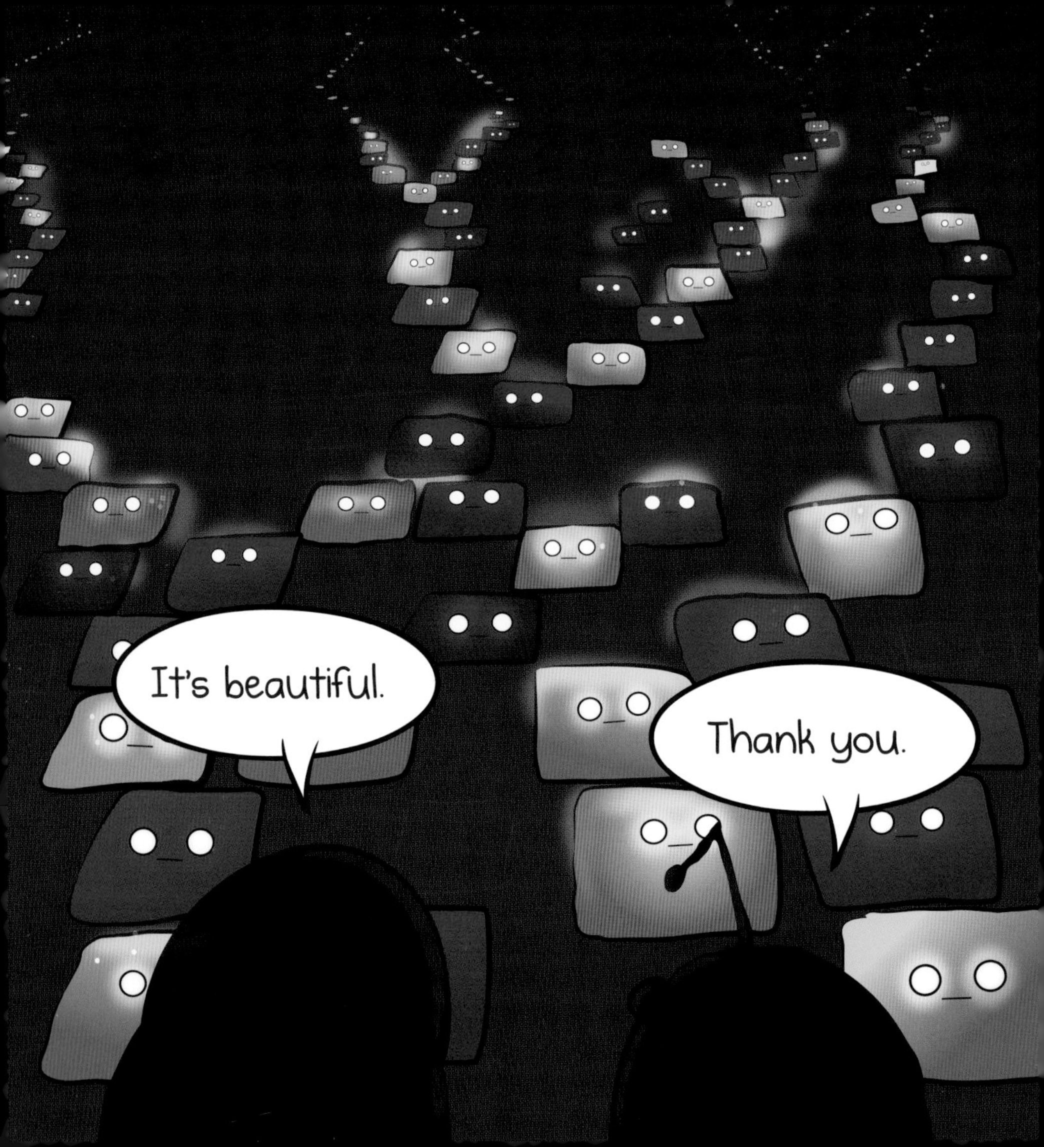
It's beautiful.
Thank you.

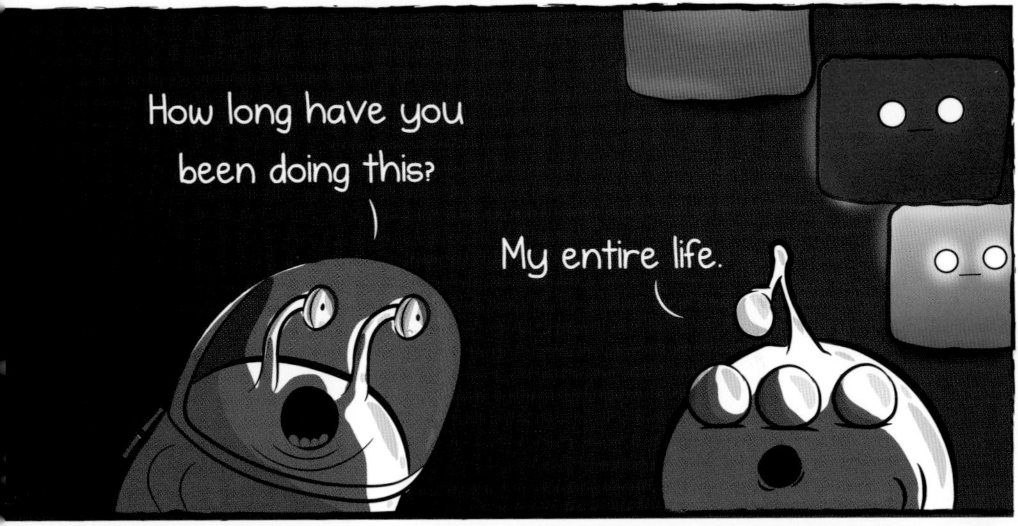
How long have you been doing this?
My entire life.

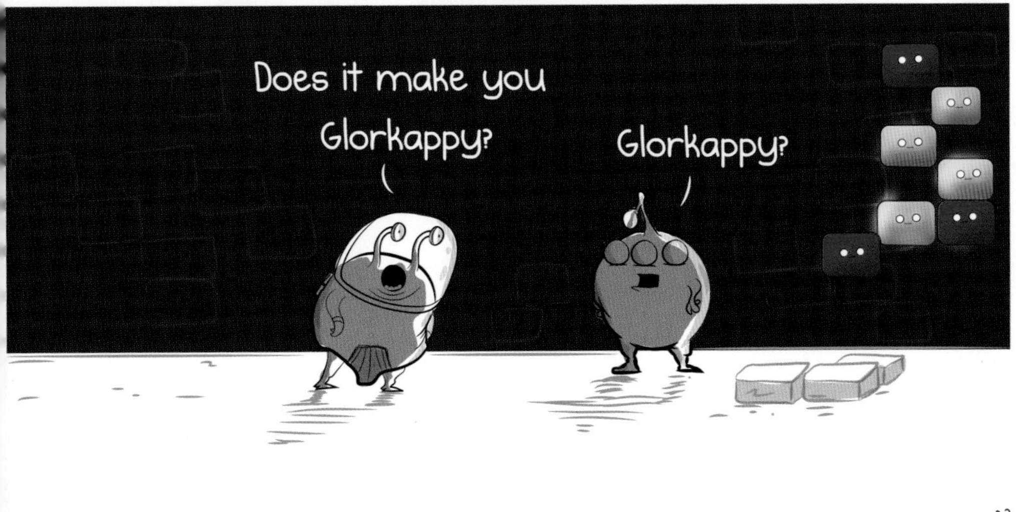
Does it make you Glorkappy?
Glorkappy?

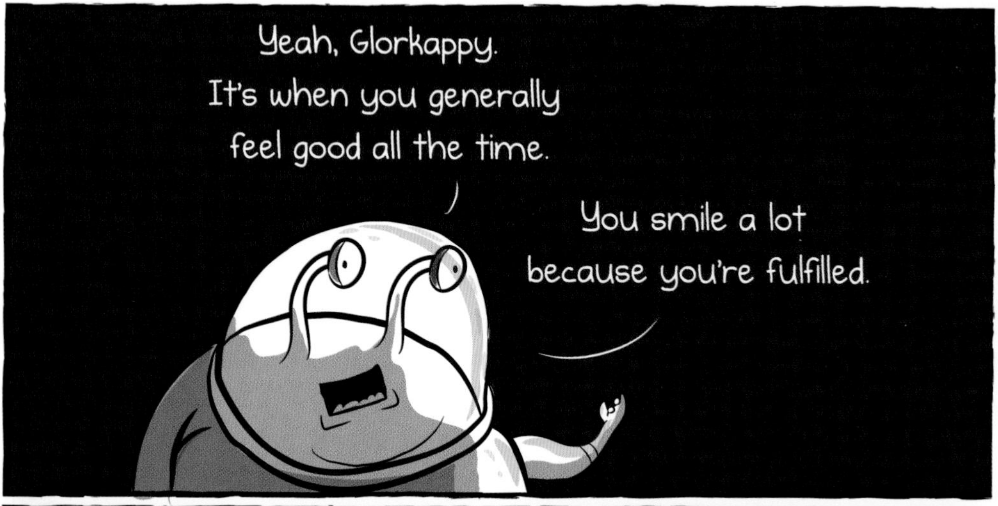
Yeah, Glorkappy.
It's when you generally feel good all the time.
You smile a lot because you're fulfilled.

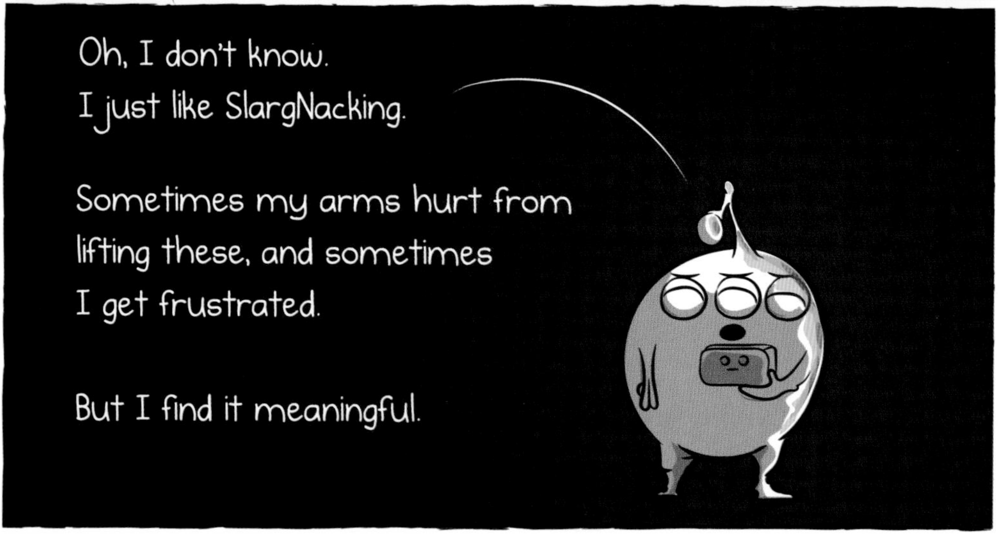
Oh, I don't know.
I just like SlargNacking.
Sometimes my arms hurt from lifting these, and sometimes I get frustrated.
But I find it meaningful.

I guess I never really thought about it until now.

I guess I'm not all that Glorkappy.

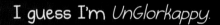

I guess I'm *UnGlorkappy.*

PLOP!

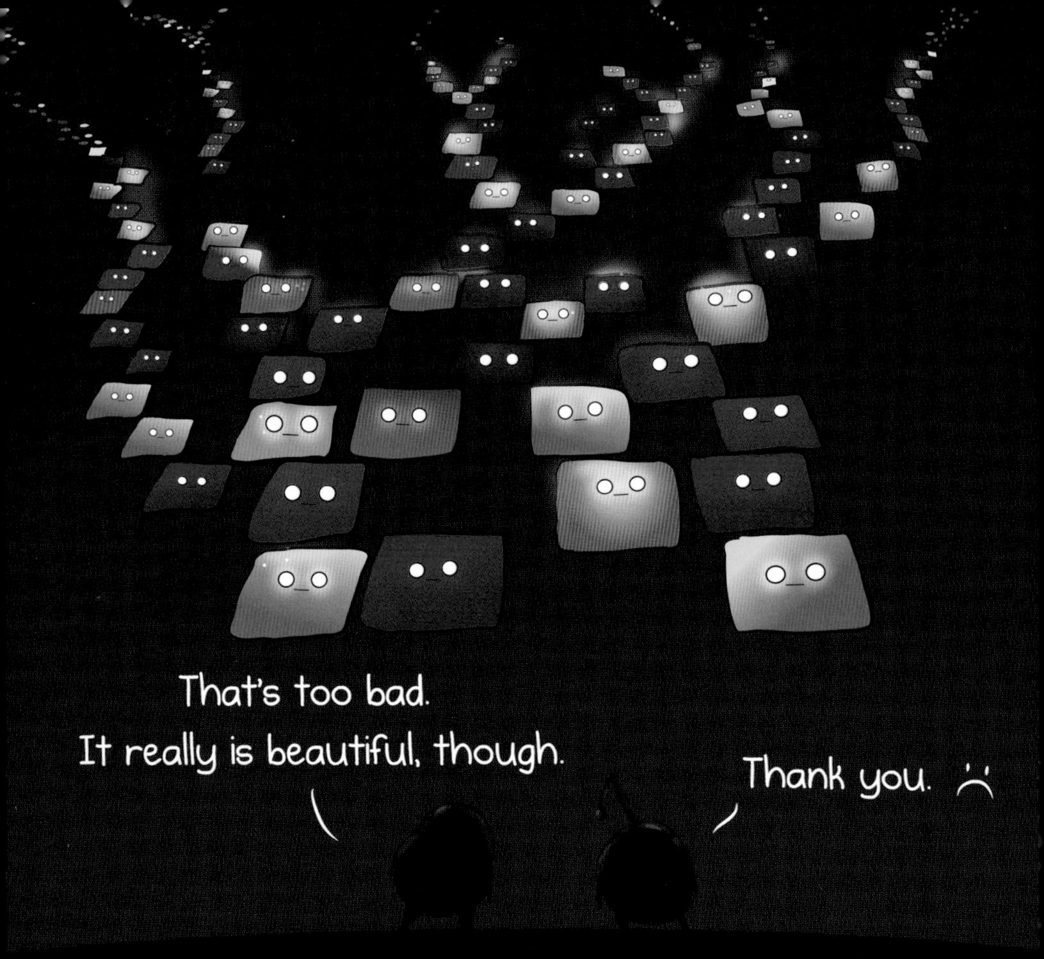
That's too bad.
It really is beautiful, though.
Thank you.

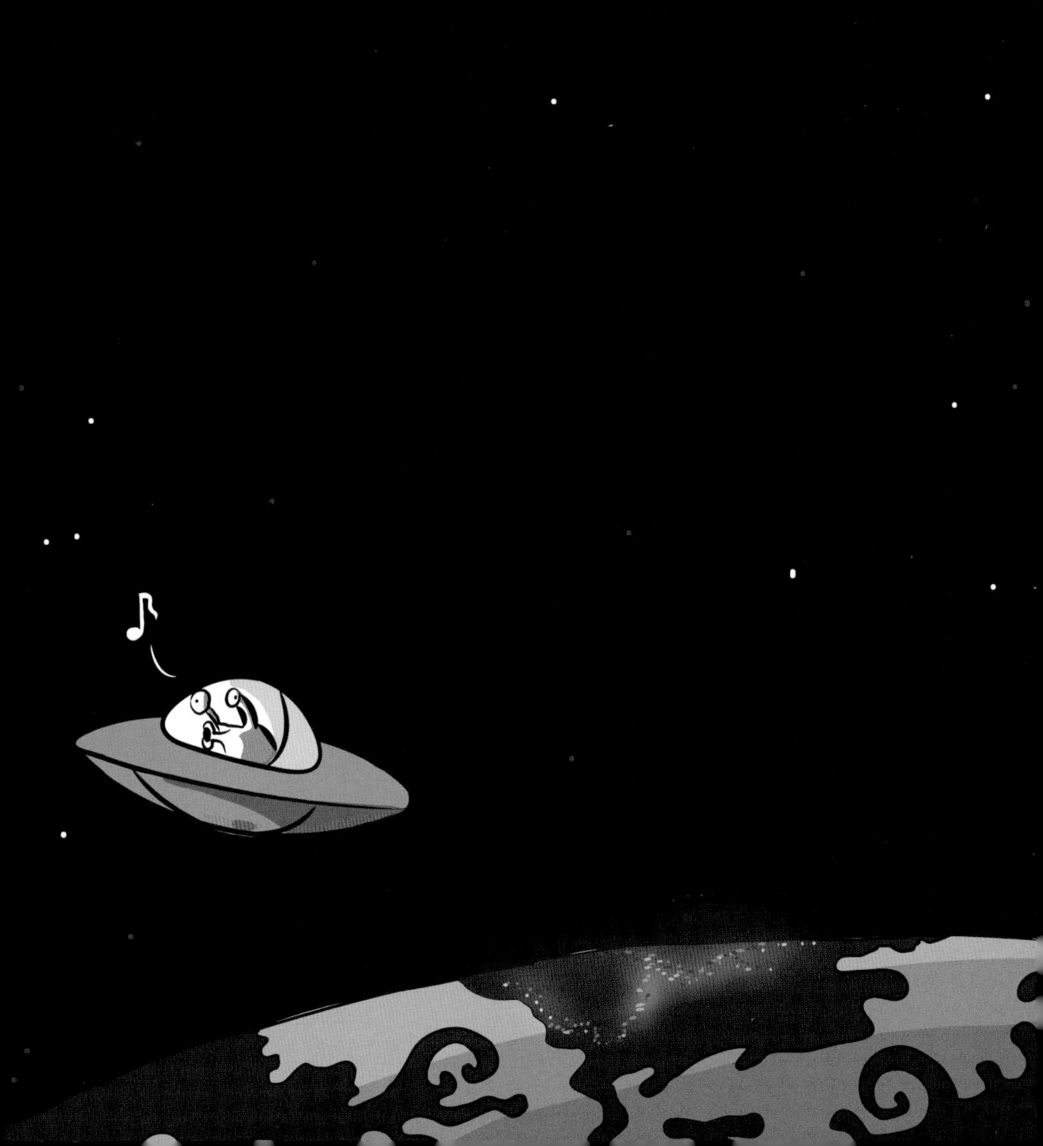

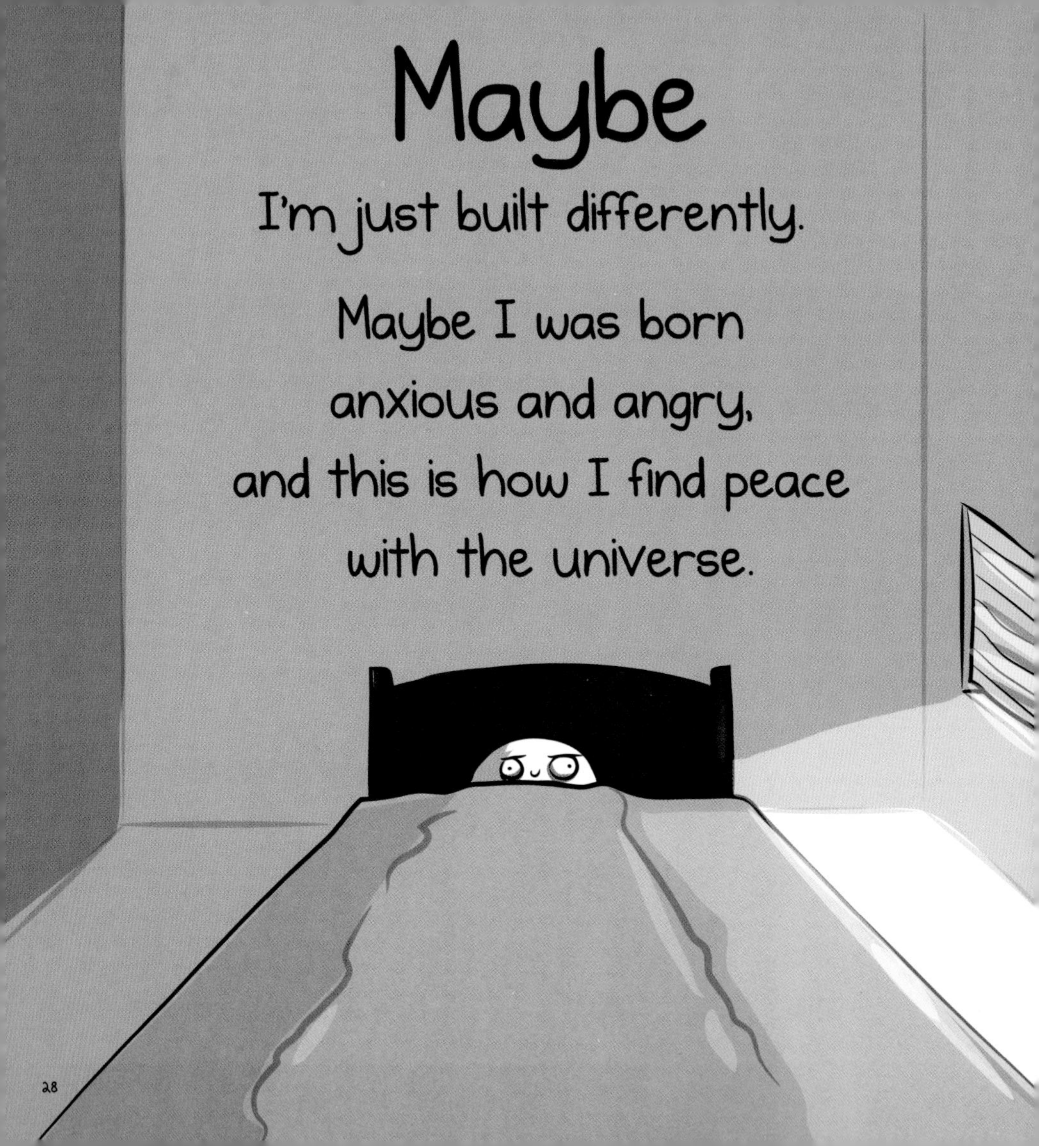
Maybe
I'm just built differently.
Maybe I was born anxious and angry, and this is how I find peace with the universe.

Maybe I truly am miserable, and everyone else is feeling something I'm not.

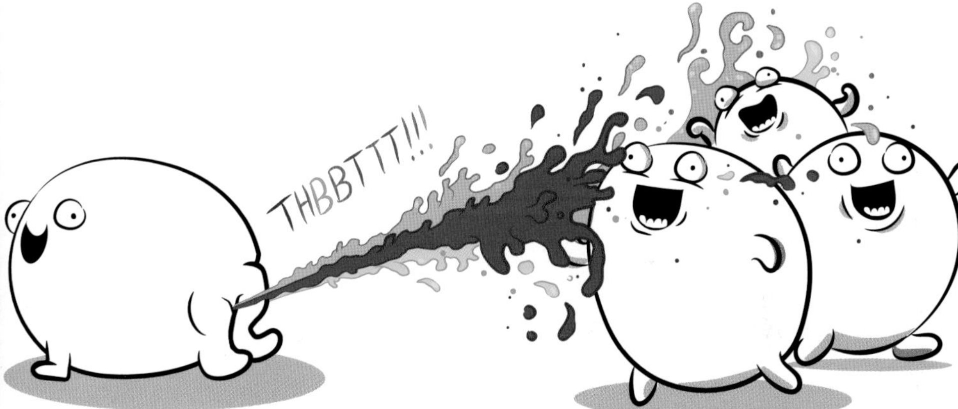
THBBTTTT!!!

Or maybe they're all full of crap.

It's irrelevant.
Because I'm not happy,
and I don't pretend to be.

Instead,
I'm busy.
I'm interested.
I'm *fascinated.*

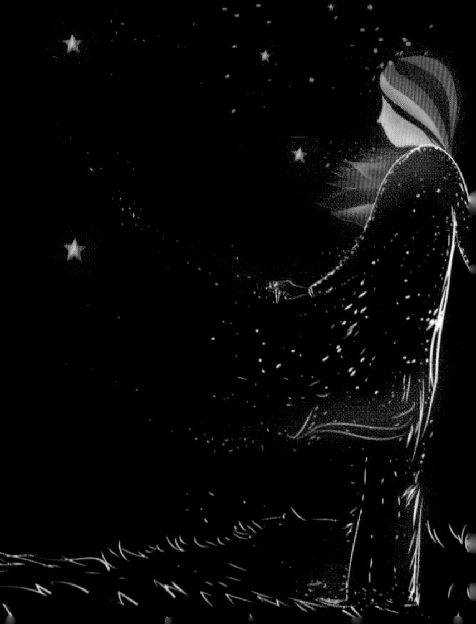

I do things that are meaningful to me,
even if they don't make me "happy."

This should work.

I run.

I run fifty miles at a time.

I run ultramarathons over mountains until my toenails fall off.

I run until my feet bleed
and my skin burns
and my bones scream.

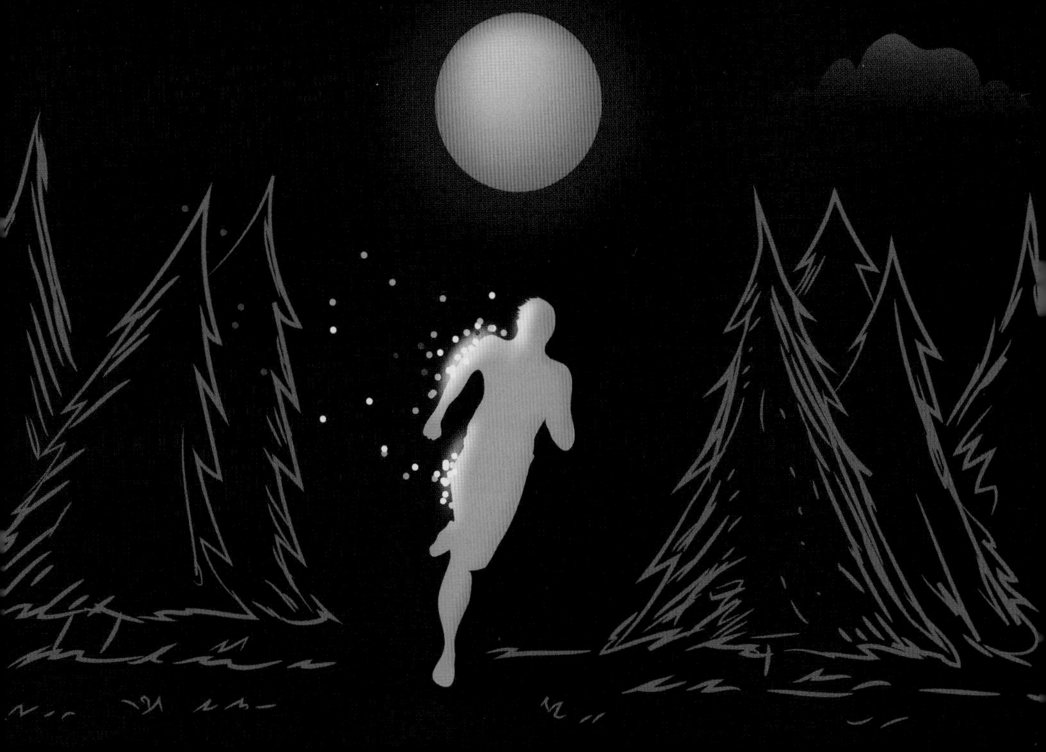

I read.

I read long, complicated books about very smart things.

And I read short, silly books about very stupid things.

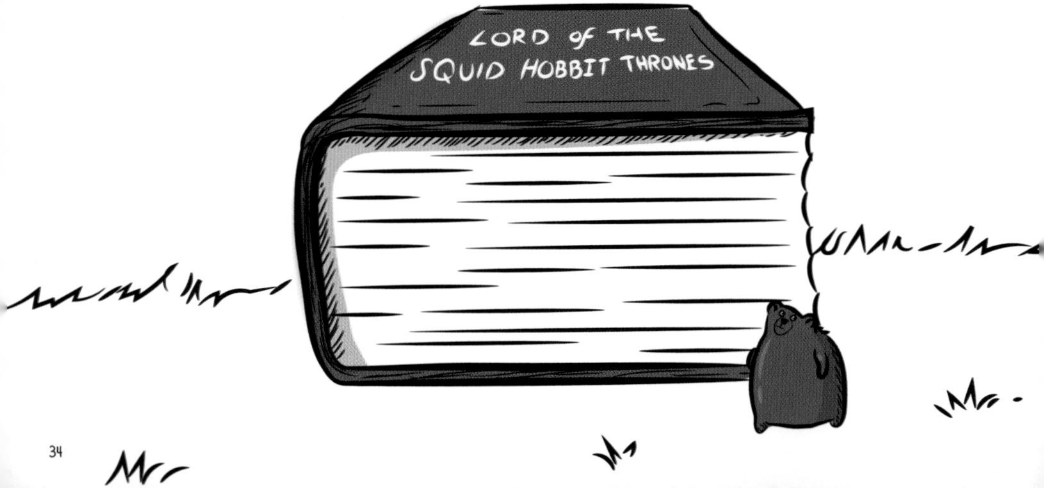
LORD of THE
SQUID HOBBIT THRONES

I read until their stories are more fascinating to me than the people actually around me.

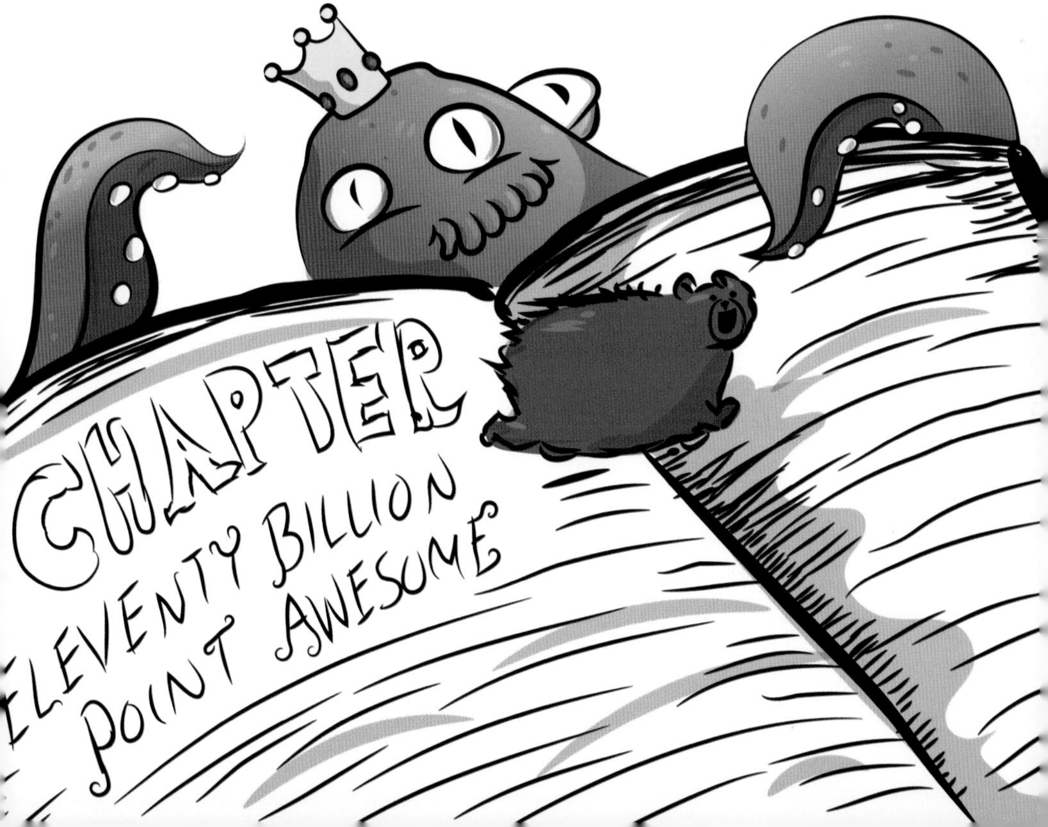

CHAPTER
ELEVENTY BILLION
POINT AWESOME

I work.

I work for twelve hours a day.

I work until I can't think straight
and I forget to feed myself and the
light outside dims to a tired glow.

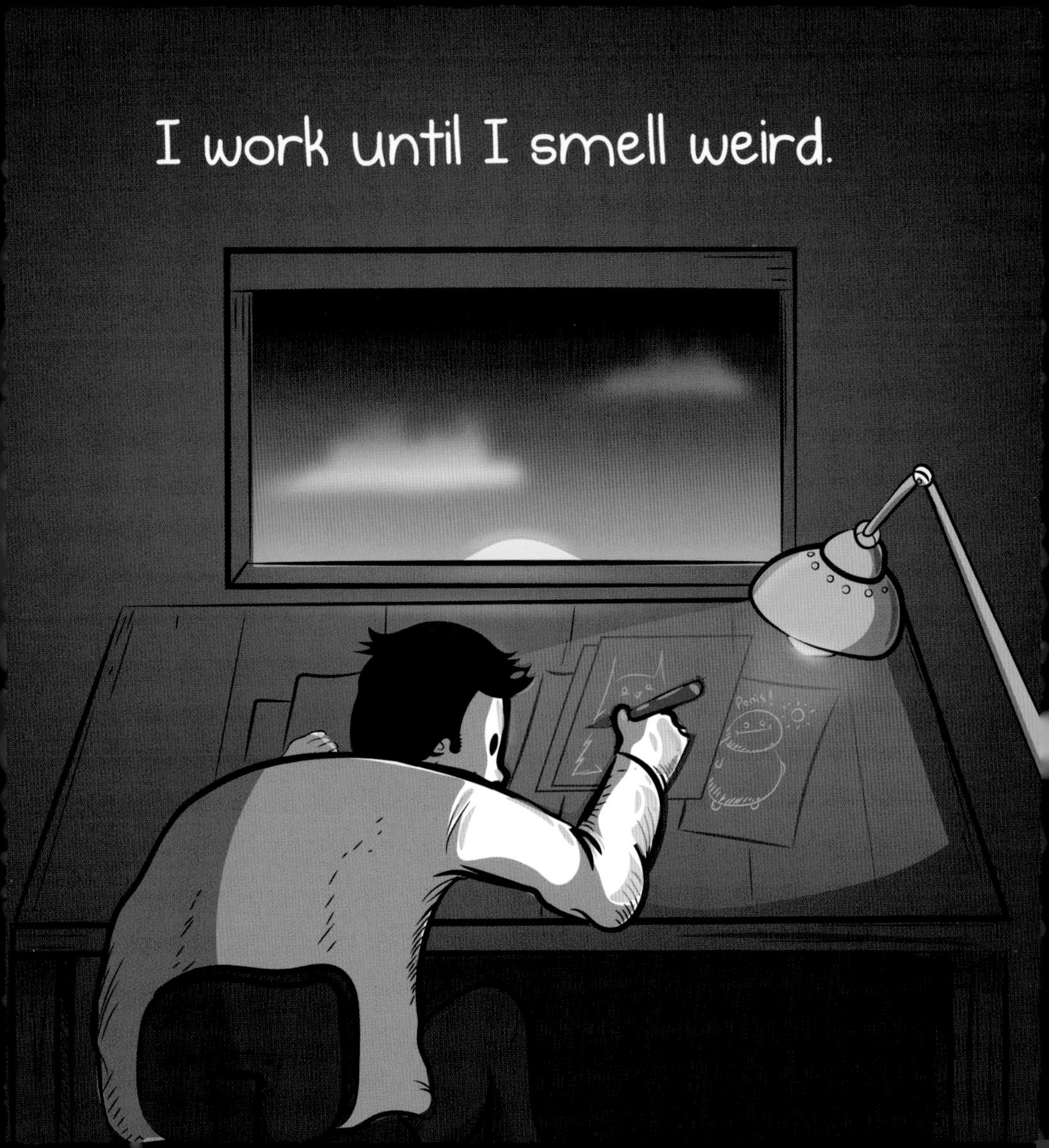
I work until I smell weird.
Penis!

When I do these things,
I'm not smiling or beaming with joy.

I'm not *happy*.

In truth, when I do these things,
I'm often suffering.

But I do them because I find them

meaningful.

I find them compelling.

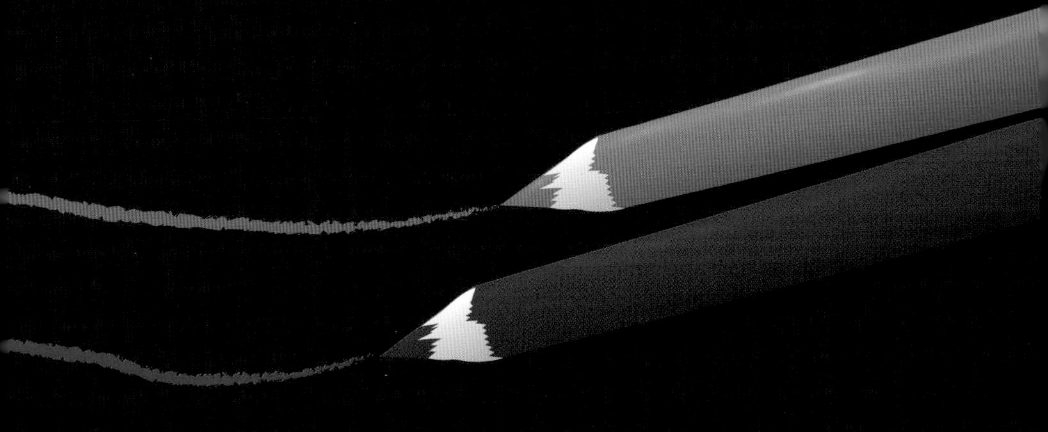

I do these things because I want to be tormented and challenged and *interested*.

I want to build things and then break them.

I want to be busy and beautiful
and brimming with
ten thousand moving parts.

I want to hurt, so that I can heal.

I'm not unhappy.
I'm just busy.
I'm *interested*.

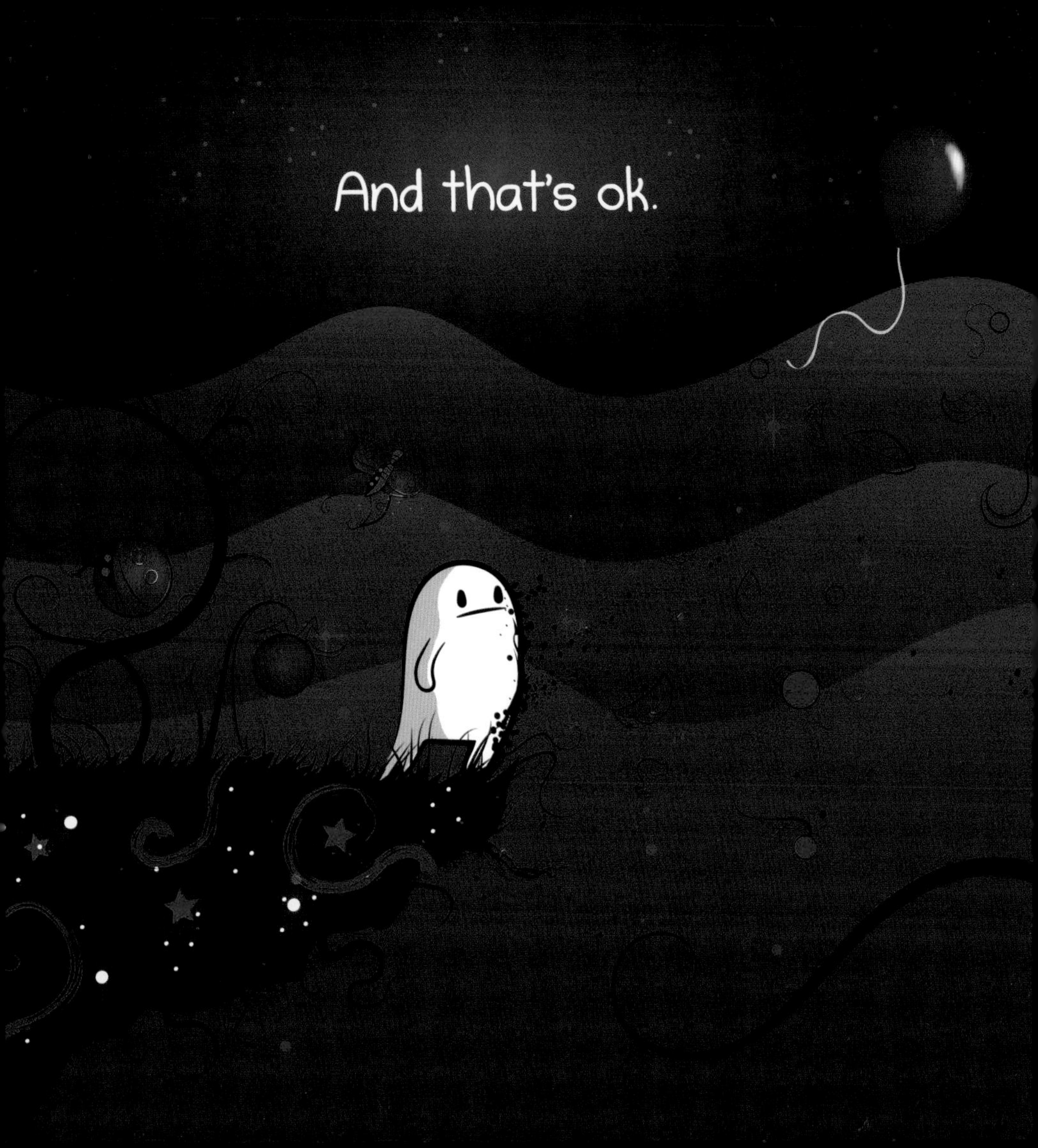
And that's ok.

About the author

This book was written and drawn by
Matthew Inman.

Matthew is the Eisner Award-winning creator of *The Oatmeal*
and the #1 *New York Times* bestselling author of
How to Tell If Your Cat Is Plotting to Kill You.
He also cocreated the card game Exploding Kittens
and founded the Beat The Blerch marathon series.

Matthew lives in Seattle, Washington,
with his two dogs, Rambo and Beatrix.

Acknowledgments and inspiration

This book was inspired by an essay from Augusten Burroughs titled
How to Live Unhappily Ever After, which can be found in the online version of
the *Wall Street Journal*. It has also been described in psychology as "flow."